The Body in Action

KU-575-613

Moving

Jillian Powell

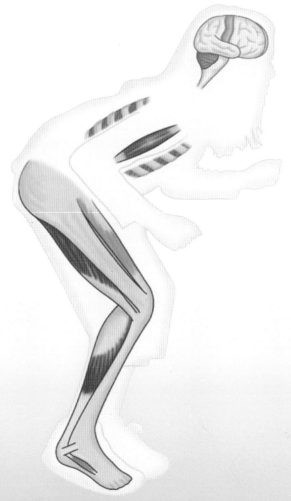

Titles in this series:
Eating
Moving
Seeing
Thinking and Feeling

Copyright © 2004 Bailey Publishing
Associates Ltd

Produced for A & C Black by
Bailey Publishing Associates Ltd
11a Woodlands
Hove BN3 6TJ

Editor: Alex Woolf
Designer: Stonecastle Graphics
Artwork: Michael Courtney
Cartoons: Peter Bull
Picture research and commissioned
photography: Ilumi Image Research
Consultant: Dr Kate Barnes

First published in 2003 by
A & C Black Publishers Ltd, 37 Soho Square,
London W1D 3QZ
www.acblack.com

All rights reserved. No part of this publication
may be reproduced or used in any form
or by any means - photographic, electronic
or mechanical, including photocopying,
recording, taping or information storage
and retrieval systems - without written
permission of the publishers.

A CIP catalogue record for this book is available
from the British Library.

ISBN 0 7136 63367

A & C Black uses paper produced with elemental
chlorine-free pulp, harvested from managed
sustainable forests.

Printed in Hong Kong
by Wing King Tong.

Picture Acknowledgements:
Acestock: 16; **Corbis:** Yann Arthus-Betrand: 9l;
Ed Bock: 27; Jim McDonald: 14; Owen Franken:
28; Wally McNamee: 22; Jose Luis-Pelaez, Inc.:
24; Kelly Mooney Photography: 10; Tom
Stewart: 5b; **Getty Images:** Brad Hitz: 5t; Brad
Martin: 29t; Ray Massey: 20; Sean Murphy: 8;
Duane Rieder: 12; Camille Tokerud: 4; David
Young-Wolff: 29b; **Science Photo Library:** 26.

DUDLEY PUBLIC LIBRARIES
L
693924   SCH
J 612.76

Contents

Moving your body

EVERY DAY, you move your body in thousands of different ways, from tiny movements such as smiling to big movements such as standing up or sitting down. When you were a baby, you could only make a few movements, such as blinking. But as you grew older, you learned lots of new ways to move, such as walking, jumping and climbing the stairs.

DID YOU KNOW?

It is your brain that makes all your movements happen. Every second it takes in information from your senses and sends out orders to tell your body to move. Sometimes you don't have time to think about it, such as when a bee comes too close.

Babies start moving around by crawling. Later, they learn to stand up and take their first steps.

You choose to make some movements, such as putting on a sweater if you feel cold. Other movements happen without you thinking about them, such as moving your mouth to talk or eat. You even move around in bed when you are sleeping!

It is good fun to run and jump, and good for your body too. These kinds of movements help you to grow strong bones.

To climb stairs you need to use balance and coordination skills.

Using your bones

YOUR BONES hold your body together and help you to move. Your **spine** keeps you upright and lets you bend and twist your whole body. Your leg bones help you to stand, sit, balance and walk. The bones in your arms, hands and fingers let you write, hold a book and wave to your friends.

Bones are light but very strong. They are smooth and hard on the outside, with spongy layers inside. In the centre, there is a thick jelly called **bone marrow**. Bones meet at **joints**, where they are covered by a slippery material called **cartilage**. This stops the bones rubbing against each other as you move.

DID YOU KNOW?
There are 206 bones in your skeleton and 29 of these are in your head.

Dancing helps you to grow strong bones, and to develop skills such as jumping and balancing.

Some bones are for protection and do not move, such as your **skull** which protects your brain.

Your **ribcage** protects your heart and lungs. It is flexible and moves in and out when you breathe.

Your **spine** is a string of small bones running up the length of your back. These bones let you bend and twist.

Your bones meet at your **joints**. Some joints, such as your elbow, allow movement.

Joints are protected by **cartilage** to stop the bones rubbing as you move.

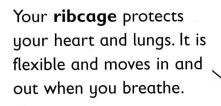

STAY HEALTHY
Your bones are growing and changing all the time. To keep them strong, you need to eat foods such as milk, yoghurt and cheese. These contain calcium and vitamin D.

The bones in your feet help you to balance and walk. You have two bones in each big toe, and three in each of your other toes.

Using your joints

THERE ARE fixed **joints** and moving joints in your skeleton. Fixed joints hold your bones tightly together. Moving joints help you to twist and bend different parts of your body. Bones are held together at the joints by **ligaments**, which are like strong, stretchy bands.

Moving joints work in different ways. Your elbows and knees bend in only one direction, just like a door hinge. Your hips and your shoulders are more like bowls. Your leg and arm bones can sit inside them and swivel in all directions. Your wrists and ankles let you move your hands and feet from side to side as well as backwards and forwards.

STAY HEALTHY

Joints work best when they are being used every day. As people get older and move less, their joints can get stiff. Doing gentle exercises can help them to move more easily.

When you hang from a tree, your shoulder joints let your arm bones swivel inside them.

DID YOU KNOW?

Some people are double-jointed. This means they have joints that can bend in unusual ways, such as a thumb that can bend backwards as well as forwards.

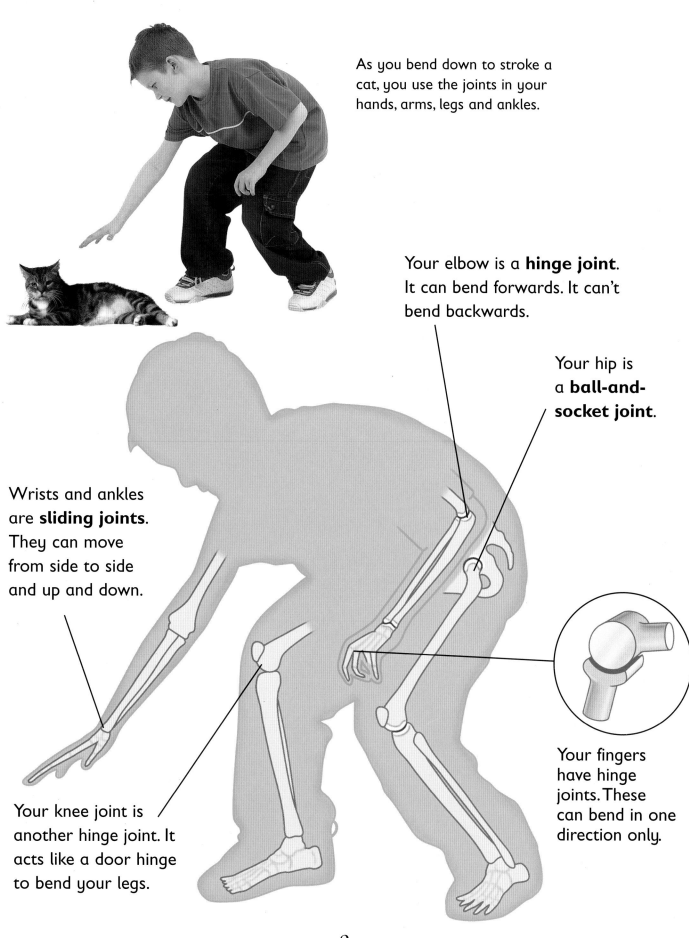

As you bend down to stroke a cat, you use the joints in your hands, arms, legs and ankles.

Your elbow is a **hinge joint**. It can bend forwards. It can't bend backwards.

Your hip is a **ball-and-socket joint**.

Wrists and ankles are **sliding joints**. They can move from side to side and up and down.

Your fingers have hinge joints. These can bend in one direction only.

Your knee joint is another hinge joint. It acts like a door hinge to bend your legs.

Deciding to move

YOUR BRAIN controls every movement in your body. When you decide to move, your brain sends signals to different parts of your body to tell them to work. These signals come from a part of the brain called the **motor area**. Another part of your brain sends out messages when you need to make lots of different movements together, such as pedalling your bike while signalling to turn a corner.

Your brain is connected to every part of your body by thousands of **nerves**. These are small bundles of fibres that work together to send messages from your brain to your body. Lots of nerves go down your **spine** to the lower part of your body.

The brain has an area that helps the body master difficult movements such as juggling.

STAY HEALTHY
You can help prevent injuries by wearing protective clothes such as helmets, elbow-pads and knee-pads when you do sports. These protect your bones and your brain.

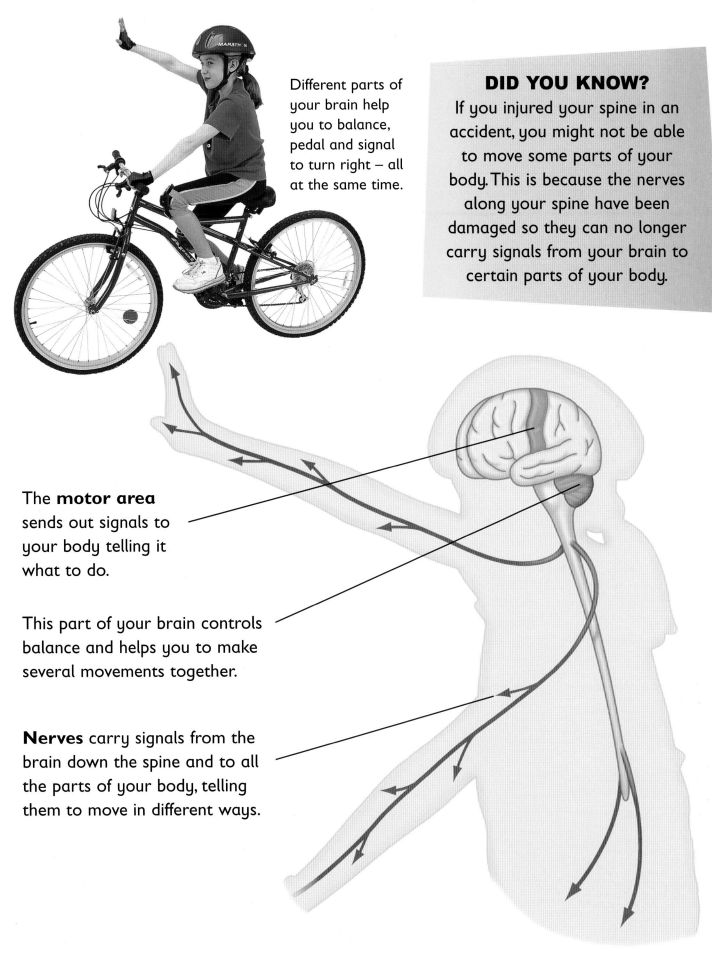

Different parts of your brain help you to balance, pedal and signal to turn right – all at the same time.

DID YOU KNOW?
If you injured your spine in an accident, you might not be able to move some parts of your body. This is because the nerves along your spine have been damaged so they can no longer carry signals from your brain to certain parts of your body.

The **motor area** sends out signals to your body telling it what to do.

This part of your brain controls balance and helps you to make several movements together.

Nerves carry signals from the brain down the spine and to all the parts of your body, telling them to move in different ways.

11

Using your muscles

YOU NEED **muscles** for every movement you make, from smiling to jumping in the air. Muscles are attached to different parts of your body, but mainly to your bones. Your brain sends signals to your muscles. These signals tell the muscles to become shorter and thicker, so that they pull on the bones and make them move.

Muscles are made from thousands of tiny fibres. They can pull but they cannot push. So muscles work in pairs or in groups to bend and straighten different parts of your body.

DID YOU KNOW?
Muscles make up nearly half the weight of your body. The smallest muscle is called the stapedius, and it is in your ear.

By exercising, this weightlifter has made his muscles grow very big.

Muscles grow and get stronger when you exercise them. You are less likely to injure your muscles if you do stretching exercises to warm them up before doing any sports.

The **biceps muscle** in your upper arm shortens to bend your arm as you throw a ball.

When you raise your arm to throw the ball, the **deltoid muscle** in your shoulder shortens and lifts the bone in your upper arm.

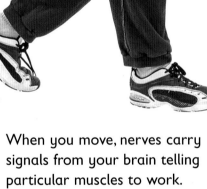

When you move, nerves carry signals from your brain telling particular muscles to work. When you stop moving, your muscles relax again.

The **thigh muscles** in this leg tighten to help you keep your balance.

Calf muscles shorten to bend this leg and pull it backwards.

13

About your lungs

YOUR MUSCLES need **oxygen** to make them work. There is lots of oxygen in the air. As you breathe you suck the air into your **lungs**, which are spongy organs inside your chest. Your lungs get bigger as you breathe in. The oxygen in the air then passes from your lungs into your blood, and is pumped around the body by your heart.

As you breathe out, the air leaves your lungs and they get smaller. This stale air now contains **carbon dioxide**. It travels along your **windpipe** and out of your mouth and nose.

DID YOU KNOW?
When you are resting, you take one breath about every three or four seconds. When you are exercising you can breathe in twice every second, and take in 15 times as much air!

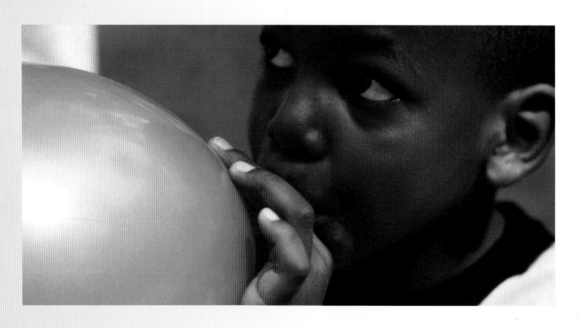

As this boy blows up a balloon, his breathing muscles push the air out of his lungs.

Sports like football help to keep your heart and lungs strong and healthy.

STAY HEALTHY

You can keep your lungs healthy by exercising every day and never smoking. Smoking damages your lungs. People who smoke find breathing more difficult when they exercise.

Oxygen passes from your **lungs** into your blood, which is then pumped around the body.

When you breathe in, fresh air and oxygen travel in through your nose and mouth, then down through your **windpipe**.

Your **diaphragm** moves downward, so that your lungs can expand and fill with air.

Muscles in your **ribcage** contract to make your ribs move outwards.

15

About your heart

YOUR HEART pumps blood around your body. When you run, jump or play any sport, your **muscles** have to work harder. They need more **oxygen**, which is carried around your body in your blood. Your heart has to beat faster to pump the blood more quickly to your muscles.

When you are resting, your heart beats about 70 times a minute. When you are exercising, it can beat twice as fast and pump three times as much blood and oxygen with each beat.

DID YOU KNOW?

You can tell how fast your heart is pumping blood by taking your pulse. Place two fingers on the inside of your wrist. Count the number of beats for 15 seconds, then multiply by four to find your pulse rate. (Your pulse rate is your heart rate over a minute.)

When you exercise, the vessels that carry blood under your skin get wider so more blood can flow through them. This can make you look pink!

STAY HEALTHY

You can keep your heart healthy by not eating too many fatty foods. These leave fat deposits behind, so your heart has to work extra hard to pump blood through them.

Your brain tells your heart how fast it needs to beat every minute of your life. When you are exercising, your brain tells your heart to beat more quickly.

3. The heart pumps your blood out with such force it can go all around your body carrying oxygen.

4. When the blood has been all round your body, it comes back to your heart. This time it goes into the right side.

6. The heart pumps your blood back to your lungs to pick up more oxygen.

5. **Heart valves** open and close to keep blood flowing round your body one way.

1. Blood enters the left side of your heart. It has come from your **lungs** and is full of **oxygen**.

2. The heart has a thick wall of **muscle** that contracts to push the blood out.

Jumping

WHEN YOU jump in the air, you use your brain, heart, **lungs** and lots of different bones and **muscles**. First, you crouch down. Muscles in the backs of your **thighs** pull to bend your legs. Muscles in your **calves** bend your ankles ready for take-off. Arm muscles pull to bend your arms and help you balance.

You use your lungs to take a deep breath. As you jump, your heart beats faster to pump **oxygen** to your muscles. Your brain tells the muscles in the front of your thighs to extend your legs. It tells muscles at the backs of your arms to extend your arms.

As you get ready for take-off, muscles pull to bend your arms and legs.

In mid-air, different muscles pull to extend your arms and legs, and to keep you balanced.

DID YOU KNOW?
High-jump athletes exercise to make the muscles in their thighs and calves extra strong. They also watch computer models of their jumping to see how to improve.

As you get ready to jump, the **biceps muscle** pulls to bend your arm and help you to balance.

As you jump up, the **triceps muscle** pulls to straighten your arm.

Your brain sends signals to the muscles in your arms and legs.

Muscles in your **ribcage** contract so that your lungs can stretch and take in more air.

Hamstring muscles pull to bend your legs at the knees.

Calf muscles shorten to bend your legs at the ankles.

Muscles in your feet push off from the ground.

Quadriceps muscles pull to straighten your legs in mid-air.

19

Pulling a face

YOUR FACE shows whether you feel happy, angry, surprised, scared or sad. You have thirty different **muscles** in your face to make all these movements. The muscles on either side of your mouth help you talk, chew food and smile. When you raise your eyebrows or frown, you use the muscles in your forehead.

The muscles in your eyelids let you open and shut your eyes and blink. You blink about five times every minute of the day. This helps to stop your eyes getting dry and gets rid of dust. That means you blink about 300 times an hour and more than 5,000 times a day!

DID YOU KNOW?
You use only 17 muscles to smile, but twice as many to frown!

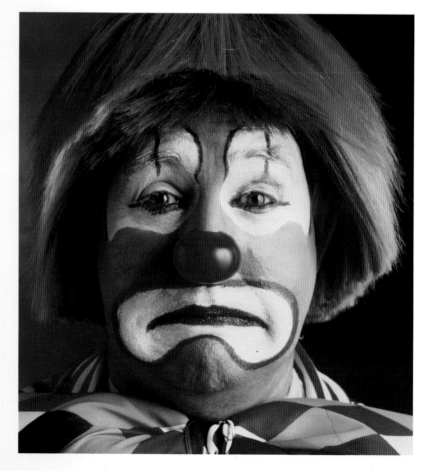

This clown's face shows how muscles pull your mouth down when you are feeling sad.

Face muscles are attached to each other, rather than to your bones, so you can move them in hundreds of different ways. You use many of them when you show surprise.

When you are surprised, **muscles** in your forehead raise your eyebrows.

There are muscles all around your eyes. These pull your eyes wide open.

Muscles all around your lips work together to pull your lips apart when you shout or gasp.

These muscles below your chin make your jaw drop.

21

Balancing

YOUR LEGS and feet help you to balance so that you can stand up without toppling over. When you stand on one foot, your body has to work even harder to balance. Your brain receives signals from your eyes, ears, **muscles** and **joints**, and decides which muscles need to work for you to stay upright.

Your ears also help you to balance. When you move your head, fluid deep inside your ear moves tiny hairs. These send signals to your brain to tell it that your head is moving. Your brain then sends signals to your muscles to keep you steady.

Gymnasts can learn to balance even when they are doing tricky moves like jumping and landing on a beam.

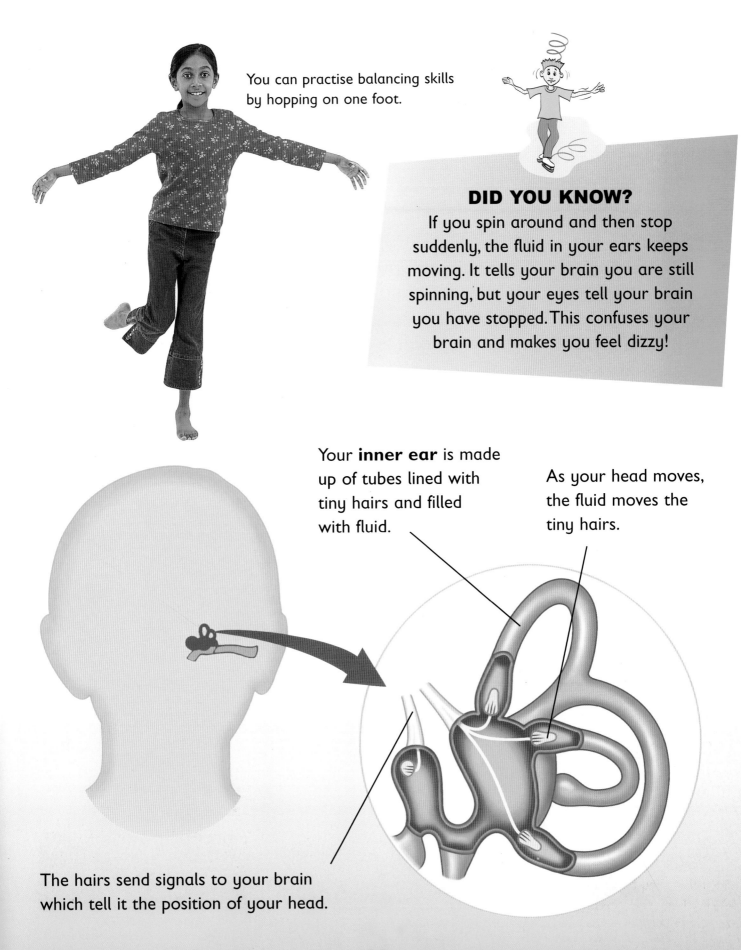

You can practise balancing skills by hopping on one foot.

DID YOU KNOW?
If you spin around and then stop suddenly, the fluid in your ears keeps moving. It tells your brain you are still spinning, but your eyes tell your brain you have stopped. This confuses your brain and makes you feel dizzy!

Your **inner ear** is made up of tubes lined with tiny hairs and filled with fluid.

As your head moves, the fluid moves the tiny hairs.

The hairs send signals to your brain which tell it the position of your head.

23

Reflex actions

IF YOU pick up a hot saucepan, or if a wasp is about to sting you, your body reacts immediately. There is not enough time for signals to travel to your brain and your brain to give orders to your body. Instead, signals flash from your skin to your **spine**, then straight back to your muscles to tell you to pull away from the danger. This is called a **reflex action** and it happens very quickly.

Reflex actions help you to avoid injury, such as being burnt, stung or hit. But coughing and sneezing are also reflex actions. These help you to get rid of dust or germs in your nose, throat and lungs.

DID YOU KNOW?
Shivering is a reflex action. When you are cold, your muscles try to make more heat by working on their own, making you shiver all over.

Doctors can test your reflexes by gently tapping just under your knee. This makes your foot kick out on its own.

A reflex action makes you drop a hot plate before you have time to think about it.

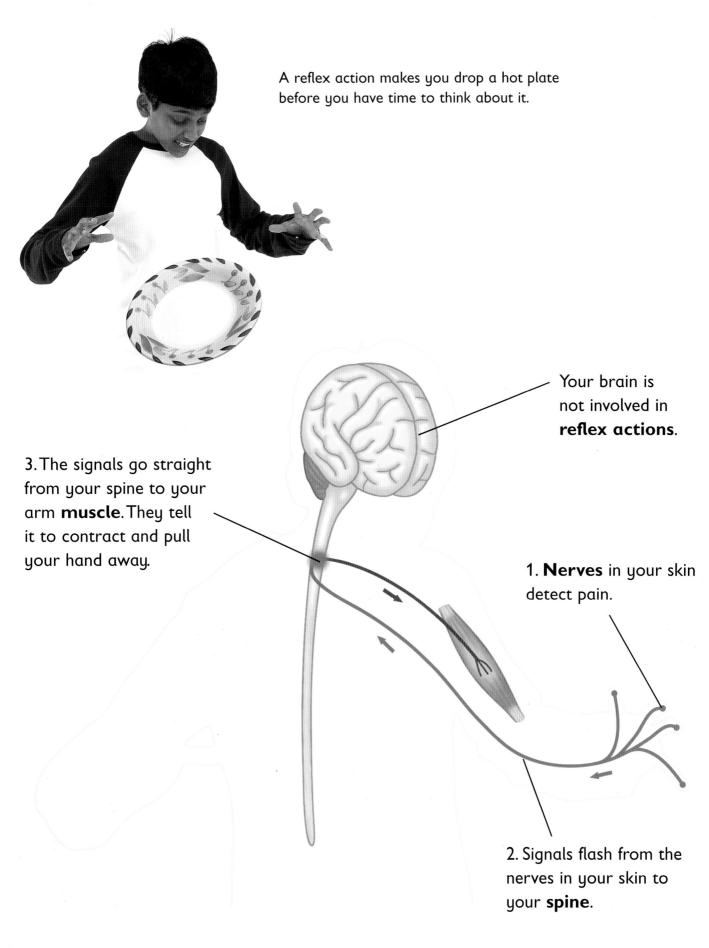

Your brain is not involved in **reflex actions**.

3. The signals go straight from your spine to your arm **muscle**. They tell it to contract and pull your hand away.

1. **Nerves** in your skin detect pain.

2. Signals flash from the nerves in your skin to your **spine**.

Injuries

IF YOU stretch **muscles** too far, you can strain them or even tear them, so they feel painful and swollen. New muscle soon grows to heal the tear if you rest. **Ligaments** and **tendons** can also be torn. These take longer to heal and may need an operation.

If you have a bad fall, you can break a bone. A doctor will take an X-ray to see if the bone can heal on its own, or if it needs an operation. Sometimes a metal pin is put into the bone to hold it in place.

DID YOU KNOW?
Children's bones mend more quickly than adult bones because their new bone grows faster.

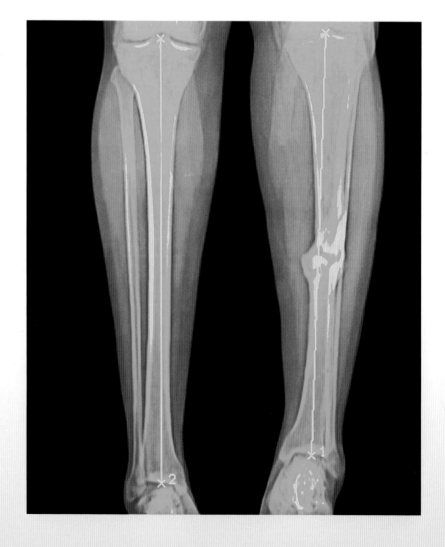

This x-ray shows where a shin bone in the leg has fractured.

A plaster cast keeps the broken bone steady until it heals.

3. New blood vessels grow to feed the new bone.

2. New bone grows to heal over the **fracture**.

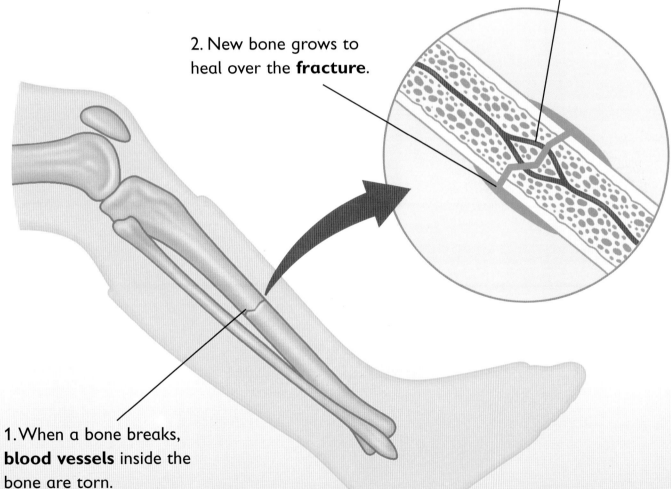

1. When a bone breaks, **blood vessels** inside the bone are torn.

Getting energy

YOUR BODY needs energy to move. You get energy from foods that contain **carbohydrates**, **fats** or **proteins**. Your body breaks down the food and turns it into a kind of sugar, which is carried in your blood to your muscles. We use units called **kilocalories** to measure the energy we get from food.

Carbohydrates such as pasta give marathon runners energy for long races.

STAY HEALTHY

Fatty foods, such as burgers and cakes, are rich in energy but they should only provide about a third of all the kilocalories in your diet. Carbohydrates, such as pasta, bread and cereals, are a healthier source of energy and contain **vitamins** and **minerals** too.

Starchy carbohydrate foods, such as pasta and cereals, release energy slowly to give you stamina. Marathon runners often eat pasta before a race. Sugary carbohydrates break down more quickly. So, you get a short burst of energy from foods such as chocolate bars.

DID YOU KNOW?
Your body stores energy as fat. When you exercise, your body burns fat to release kilocalories of energy.

The energy you use depends on your age and how active you are. Children need extra energy to help them grow.

When you exercise, your body uses stored carbohydrates and fats to give you energy.

Glossary

ball-and-socket joints Joints that move in all directions.

biceps An upper arm muscle that bends your elbow.

blood vessels Tubes which carry blood around your body.

bone marrow A jelly-like substance inside your bones.

calf The fleshy part at the back of your leg, below the knee.

carbohydrates Energy food containing starches or sugars, including bread, cakes and pasta.

carbon dioxide A gas in the air which passes out of your lungs when you breathe out.

cartilage A rubbery material that covers your bones where they meet at joints.

deltoid The muscle that covers your shoulder joint.

diaphragm A curved muscle at the bottom of your lungs.

fats Energy food found in animal and dairy products such as meat and cream, and in vegetable oils.

fracture A break in a bone.

hamstring muscles Muscles at the back of your thigh that bend your knee.

heart valves Flaps at the entrances of your heart which keep blood flowing round the body one way.

hinge joints Joints that move in only one direction.

inner ear The part of your ear which helps with balance.

joints Places such as your elbow where your bones meet and are held together.

kilocalorie A unit for measuring energy in food.

ligaments Strong, stretchy bands holding bones together.

lungs Spongy organs in your ribcage used for breathing.

motor area Part of the brain which sends out signals to tell your body to move

muscles Tissues that move different parts of your body.

nerves Tiny bundles of fibres that carry signals between the brain and other parts of your body.

oxygen A gas in the air which your body uses to breathe.

proteins A type of food which gives you energy and helps you grow, including meat, cheese and nuts.

quadriceps A muscle at the front of your thigh that contracts to straighten your leg.

reflex action An action such as a sneeze that happens without involving your brain.

ribcage The set of curved bones in your chest called ribs that protect your lungs and other vital organs.

skull The bony part of your head that protects the brain.

sliding joints Joints that move backwards and forwards and from side to side.

spine The string of bones down your back.

tendon A tough band of fibres that connects your muscles to your bones.

thigh The top of your leg between your knee and your hip.

triceps An upper arm muscle that straightens the elbow.

vitamins and minerals Substances that your body needs from food to stay healthy.

windpipe The tube that joins your throat to your lungs.

Useful information

Books

Blood, Bones and Body Bits by Nick Arnold, Tony de Saulles (Scholastic Hippo, 1996)

Eyewitness Guide 87: The Human Body (Dorling Kindersley, 1998)

How Does Exercise Affect Me? by Judy Sadgrove (Hodder Wayland, 1999)

Inside the Body by Sally Morgan (Kingfisher, 1997)

Understanding Your Muscles and Bones by Rebecca Treays (Usborne, 1997)

CD rom

Become a Human Body Explorer (Dorling Kindersley, 2000)

Websites

www.bbc.co.uk/health/kids
BBC site with a 'body tour' and lots of information on how the body works.

www.smartplay.net
A website which gives information on sports and recreational injuries and how to prevent them.

www.cdc.gov/powerfulbones
A site all about healthy bones.

www.kidshealth.com
Lots of information on the body and health.

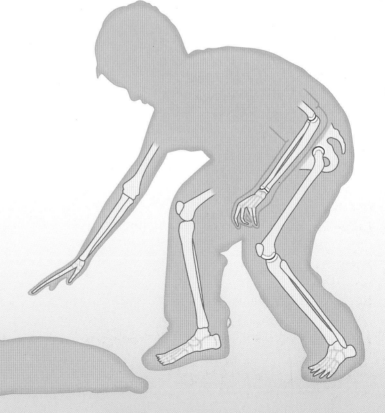

Index